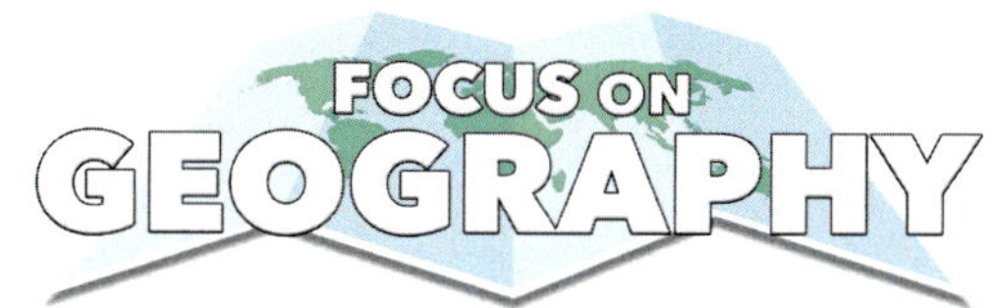

Focus on South Korea

Heather C. Hudak

Crabtree Classroom
crabtreebooks.com

Crabtree Publishing

crabtreebooks.com 800-387-7650

In Canada: We acknowledge the financial support of the Government of Canada through the Canada Book Fund for our publishing activities.

Published in Canada
Crabtree Publishing
616 Welland Avenue
St. Catharines, Ontario
L2M 5V6

Published in the United States
Crabtree Publishing
347 Fifth Avenue
Suite 1402-145
New York, NY 10016

Author: Heather C. Hudak
Series research and development: Janine Deschenes
Editorial director: Kathy Middleton
Editor: Janine Deschenes
Proofreader: Roseann Biederman
Design: Tammy McGarr
Production manager: Candice Campbell
Prepress technician: Katherine Kantor

Hardcover: 978-1-0396-6328-2
Paperback: 978-1-0396-6377-0
Ebook (pdf): 978-1-0396-6820-1
Epub: 978-1-0396-8560-4
Read-along: 978-1-0396-8609-0
Audio book: 978-1-0396-6869-0

Printed in the U.S.A./072025/CP20250721

Library and Archives Canada Cataloguing in Publication Available at Library and Archives Canada

Library of Congress Cataloging-in-Publication Data
Available at the Library of Congress

Image Credits:

Creative Commons
p. 12 (bottom right), p. 31 (bottom)

iStock
NGCHIYUI: p. 5 (top)

Creative Commons
Vero Villa: p. 39 (top)

Public Domain
p. 19 (bottom), p. 24 (bottom), Metropolitan Museum of Art: p. 35 (left)

Shutterstock
Sean Pavone: Roman Babakin: front cover (top left), TOC page, Guitar photographer: front cover (top middle), p. 4 (top), trabantos: p. 4 (bottom), p. 23 (top), A. Emson: p. 5 (bottom), ESB Professional: p. 9 (bottom), etspicsit: p. 11 (bottom), Takashi Images: p. 14, Savvapanf Photo: p. 15 (top), Stock for you: p. 15 (bottom), p. 28-29 (top), p. 17, FenlioQ: p. 18 (top), Everett Collection: p. 23 (bottom), Panwasin seemala: p. 24 (top), TamasV: front cover (top right), p. 26 (top), Noa_80: p. 26 (bottom), Ju Jae-young: p. 27 (top), Geewon Jung: p. 27 (middle right and bottom), NGCHIYUI: p. 30 (top), Markus Mainka: p. 30 (bottom), Sorbis: p. 31 (top), qingqing: p. 32, Oleg Zartdinov: p. 33 (top), Erik Laan: p. 34 (top), Panu Kosonen: p. 34 (bottom), Johnathan21: p. 35 (right), nuu_jeed: p. 38 (top), Debby Wong: p. 39 (bottom), Rei Imagine: p. 42 (bottom left), na_pena: p. 43, lebedev: p. 44 (top)

All other images from Shutterstock

SOUTH KOREA
SOUTH KOREA
Lily Cat
HOUSE
Talent
Cosmetic
샤라 샤라
carver korea
SINCE 1999
mint
足 マッサージ
全身マッサージ
776-8964
3F入口
占い
カフェ
道 通
사주
エステサロン
세마헤어
가온헤어
ETUDE HOUSE
SUGAR STUDIO

Contents

INTRODUCTION

Given the hustle and bustle of Seoul, the tower offers a serene setting to relax and enjoy the city's natural beauty on a clear day.

Snapshot of a Thriving City

There is nothing quite like watching the sunset from the observation deck of the YTN Seoul Tower. Located at the top of Mount Namsan in the very center of Seoul, South Korea, the tower offers panoramic views of the vibrant city. At 1,575 feet (480 m) high, Seoul Tower is one of the tallest towers in Asia. From the top, it is easy to gaze out onto the stunning landscapes that surround the crowded city below, including the mighty Han River, rolling foothills, and steep mountain slopes.

Seoul, the nation's capital, is called the 24-hour city for good reason. It is open around the clock. *Pali pali* means "hurry up" or "faster" in the Korean language, and it represents a way of life in this energetic city. People here work longer hours than just about any other place in the world.

After a long day at the office, South Koreans often treat themselves to a night out. Some take in traditional dance performances at the National Theater, attend the Korean opera at the Korea House, or go shopping at the night markets. Others prefer to hang out at a spa, shopping center, study room, Internet café, or lounge. There are also world-class restaurants, museums, and galleries for people to enjoy.

Nearly everyone who lives in South Korea is of Korean descent. As a result, most people share similar values, ways of life, and a sense of pride in their nation.

Seoul has one of the world's largest and most energy-efficient urban railway networks.

A Bustling Hub

Located in one of the most advanced countries in the world, Seoul is the technology hub of Asia. It is known for having some of the best Internet connections and cell phone coverage on the planet. The busy city is the kind of place where a new trend blows up overnight and people are always looking to produce the next big thing.

With 10 million people living in Seoul, the city is bursting at the seams. There is so little room that most people live in sky-high apartment buildings. These skyscrapers are designed to save space and squeeze more people into smaller areas. Traffic is a nightmare and causes huge amounts of air pollution. Instead, more than 7 million people a day ride public transit. Despite being crammed together, locals are known for their friendly and kind personalities. They are especially well-known for their cheerful service.

Around six out of every 10 South Koreans live in apartment buildings.

A Country Divided

Korea is a 750-mile (1,200 km) long peninsula in East Asia. It was divided into two countries after World War II: the Democratic People's Republic of Korea, or North Korea, and the Republic of Korea, or South Korea. At that time, North Korea became a **communist** country. South Korea became a **capitalist** country. Their different ways of governing led to conflicts. For this reason, the two countries were separated along the **38th parallel** by a region called the Demilitarized Zone (DMZ).

The DMZ is a 160-mile-long, 2.5-mile-wide (258 km long, 4 km wide) strip of land. It serves as a buffer between North and South Korea. No military is allowed in this area, and no one can cross the border from either country. There is heavy military on either side of the DMZ.

Three Seas

South Korea is located in the southernmost part of the Korean peninsula. The country is bordered by three seas. The East Sea, or Sea of Japan, is in the East. To the South is the South Sea, or East China Sea, and in the West is the West Sea, or Yellow Sea. The country has about 1,500 miles (2,413 km) of coastline. It has no land borders other than with North Korea.

The Demilitarized Zone is the most heavily **fortified** border in the world.

- **OFFICIAL NAME:** Republic of Korea
- **NATIONAL CAPITAL:** Seoul
- **POPULATION:** 51,672,000
- **OFFICIAL LANGUAGE:** Korean
- **LAND AREA:** 38,749 square miles (100,360 sq. km)

Signs of the Times

Many younger Koreans think of the peninsula as being tiger shaped. The tiger is a traditional symbol of wealth and power that protects the Korean people from misfortune. Older Koreans say the peninsula is shaped like a rabbit. The rabbit is a symbol of fertility and represents the bountiful harvests of South Korea's once-thriving agricultural industry.

Changing Landscape

Traditionally, South Koreans lived in small farming communities on the few parts of the country's land that are suitable for growing crops. Over time, they began to move to urban areas. Today, more than 80 percent of people live in cities. There are many large cities with populations greater than 1 million people. Major cities include Seoul, Busan, Incheon, and Daegu.

CHAPTER 1

The Land

Mountains and hills dominate the South Korean landscape. As a result, only about 30 percent of the land in South Korea is habitable, or suitable for humans to live. Wide stretches of **fertile** lowlands run along the coastline and the major rivers, especially in the western parts of the country. This is where most people live.

South Korea is the 109th largest country in the world. With an area of just 38,749 square miles (100,360 sq km), the entire country is slightly smaller than the state of Pennsylvania. Despite its limited space, South Korea has a population of nearly 52 million. That means there are about 1,294 people for every 1 square mile (499 per 1 sq km) of land. This makes South Korea one of the most **densely** populated countries in the world.

The Sobaek Mountains are the largest mountain range in South Korea, stretching southwest across the country. They reach an elevation of 6,283 feet (1,915 m).

Sharing Is Caring

Due to the country's small size, South Koreans are used to sharing their space. From being jam-packed on subways to being squished together in the grocery line, they have very little personal space. This has created a sense of connectedness known as a **collectivist culture**. This means that people in South Korea value interdependence and act in the best interest of each other. Uri is the term South Koreans use to symbolize this unity. For example, when speaking about their country, they use the words uri nara, which mean "our nation."

South Korea has extreme temperatures with four distinct seasons. Winters are cold and dry, with temperatures dipping as low as 20 degrees Fahrenheit (-5°C). The summer months are hot and humid, with average temperatures reaching well above 70 degrees Fahrenheit (25°C) in August.

More than half of South Korea's population lives in the greater Seoul **metropolitan** area.

Hiking is a favorite activity among locals, especially in Seoul, where there are many mountains and parks to explore.

Rugged Land

South Korea is a rugged country, made up of rock that formed hundreds of million years ago. Mountains and hills cover about 70 percent of South Korea. The country is home to three major mountain ranges. They are the Taebaek Mountains, the Sobaek Mountains, and the Jiri Massif. Most peaks are quite small—most stand just 3,300 feet (1,000 m) high. Rain and wind have **eroded** the mountains over millions of years. Still, living in South Korea means a lot of uphill and downhill adventures.

Volcanic Islands

South Korea's tallest peak is Mount Halla, or Hallasan, on Jeju Island. The island is the largest of more than 3,000 volcanic islands that surround the peninsula in the territory of South Korea. None of the volcanoes are active. Mount Halla rises 6,400 feet (1,950 m) into the sky. Mount Halla is one of three volcanic mountains on the Korean peninsula. The area around it is a national park. Jeju Island is also a United Nations Educational, Scientific, and Cultural Organization (UNESCO) **World Heritage Site**.

Winding Rivers

Four main rivers wind their way through South Korea: the Han, Nakdong, Yeongsan, and Geum. They begin in the mountains and flow toward the Yellow Sea or East China Sea. The longest is the Nakdong River. It stretches about 324 miles (521 km) and passes through major cities, such as Daegu and Busan. The 319-mile (514 km) long Han River that snakes through downtown Seoul is another important body of water. It was once a key trade and travel route to China via the Yellow Sea.

Today, the river is not fully passable by civilians due to the strict border between North and South Korea. However, it is one of the main sources of water for millions of South Koreans. Since the 1990s, bridges were built to make travel across the river easier. There are also many scenic walkways, paths, and parks for people to enjoy on the lower stretches of the river.

Dams were built on Han River to provide energy for hydroelectric power. The Hwacheon Dam, on the northern part of the river, is a big source of electricity in South Korea.

Natural Resources

South Korea has some of the world's largest deposits of **graphite** and **tungsten**. Other resources include lead, coal, and iron **ore**. Prior to Japanese **colonization**, the country was heavily forested. However, most trees were cut down to use as firewood or to make room for roads and railways. **Reforestation** efforts were put in place in the late 1970s to help restore South Korea's forests to their former state. Today, nearly 65 percent of the country is covered in forests.

Flora and Fauna

South Korea has a wide range of temperatures and a great deal of precipitation, making it the perfect place for many plants and animals to thrive. The country is home to about 4,500 known plant species, such as **ginseng**, Korean rose, and a type of tree called metasequoia. There are more than 18,000 animal species in South Korea. The Siberian tiger is the national animal, but it was hunted to near extinction by people who wanted to use the animal's bones in traditional medicines. Wild boar, water deer, long-tailed goral, and Korean hares are some of the other animals in Korea.

Many animals in South Korea are at risk due to pollution, hunting, and land development, including the Amur leopard, the golden eagle, lynx, and Siberian musk deer (above).

Siberian tiger

Hwangsa

Each year between March and May, strong winds blow *Hwangsa,* or "yellow dust," into South Korea from the deserts of Mongolia and northern China. The dust causes reduced visibility and air-quality issues that impact **respiratory** health. It carries viruses, fungi, bacteria, heavy metals, and industrial pollutants, such as pesticides. People are advised to stay indoors to prevent dry eyes, sore throats, and other issues. The dust can cause damage to soils and crops, and the **economy** suffers, as fewer people can leave their homes to shop, eat out, or attend outdoor events. China and South Korea are working together to help reduce the dust. One way they are doing so is by planting trees to prevent further **desertification**.

People protect themselves by wearing protective masks and glasses, by running air purifiers in their homes, and by thoroughly washing dust off food before cooking it.

Yellow dust storms have been increasing in length each year due to desertification, disrupting life for South Koreans.

Working the Land

At one time, agriculture was the main source of income in South Korea. Fields were divided into tiny plots. People worked hard to prepare the land and harvest crops by hand or using animal power. Today, farming is much less common. Most of the population in rural communities is aging. People are not as able to work the land as they once were.

Rural Life

Smaller rural villages are found throughout the river valleys and coastal lowlands of South Korea. Communities often form in clusters at the base of foothills, which help shield them from harsh winds. Homes tend to be more spread out in mountain regions. Since the mid-1900s, more people have moved to cities. Rural lifestyles are fast becoming a thing of the past, and traditional ways of life practiced in smaller communities are being lost. For instance, traditional farming families were large, and there were many children to help work the land. Today, many South Koreans choose to have only one child or even none at all.

While some traditional markets are being replaced by big box retail chains and online shopping, it is still common to find markets throughout the major cities in South Korea. There, vendors sell food, clothing, medicine, and other goods.

Flood Zone

In addition to its extreme temperatures, South Korea has seasonal monsoons, typhoons, and cyclones. Climate change has led to heavier rainfalls and more severe storms across South Korea. It is one of the top 20 countries at risk of rising sea levels due to **storm surge** and flooding. This has an especially big impact on South Koreans since most live near coastlines. Flooding can cause severe damage to homes and infrastructure, such as water, sewage, and electricity services, roads, hospitals, schools, and businesses. About 80 percent of property damage from natural disasters is the result of flooding. Typhoons bring destructive winds that also cause severe damage. Most modern structures are made from reinforced concrete that is resistant to flooding and strong winds. South Korea has also invested in strategies to reduce the impact of flooding. They include increased sewer capacity, underground tanks for rainwater storage, flood forecasting models, levees, dams, and pumping facilities.

Monsoon season in South Korea, which brings heavy, dangerous rain, generally lasts for two to six weeks, starting in mid-June or early July. As much as 60 percent of the country's annual precipitation falls during this time.

This park in Seoul is completely underwater due to the Han River flooding in early August 2020.

CHAPTER 2

Becoming South Korea

People have been living on the Korean peninsula for millions of years. They likely migrated to the area from Siberia and the Manchurian region, of what is now northeastern China, about 4,000 years ago. These ancient inhabitants lived along the coastlines and survived off the land. They hunted animals and gathered edible plants. Over time, they began to settle in clans and form farming communities. They also developed the Korean language. Pottery and other artifacts from this era show these early peoples shared a similar culture and way of life as other ancient peoples who lived in this part of Asia at the time.

Tribal States

Eventually, the most powerful clan leaders merged many clans together. As a result, Korean **tribal states** began to take shape around the first century C.E. Buyeo was one of these tribal states. It spread from Manchuria to the northern part of the Korean peninsula. South of the Han River, there were large groups of small states. They included Mahan, Jinhan, and Byeonhan. Tens of thousands of households belonged to each of these mini states. They were collectively known as the Samhan, or the Three Han States. Their territory spanned from the Sungari basin, in present-day China, to the southern part of the Korean peninsula.

Ancient Korean pottery, such as these bowls and jars, was brown in color, flat bottomed, and carved with patterns such as zigzags and comb-like lines. They are similar to the style of Chinese pottery around the same time.

Three Kingdoms

After some time, the tribal states began to unite. They became the Three Kingdoms of Koguryo in the North, Paekche in the Southwest, and Silla in the Southeast. The Gaya **confederation** at the southern tip of the Korean peninsula was also an important force at the time. The Three Kingdoms and Gaya were in constant conflict with one another. They also formed **alliances** with each other, as well as with China and Japan, which were the two main powers in the region at that time. These alliances often shifted and changed. Finally, in 676 C.E., Silla defeated its rivals with help from China. It then created the Unified Silla Kingdom in 668 C.E.

During the Three Kingdoms era, Buddhist temples were built across South Korea. Many were built in the mountains, such as this one located near Mt. Bonghwang. In the mountains, worshippers could be closer to nature and remove themselves from everyday life.

Unified Silla Kingdom

The Unified Silla Kingdom was the first **dynasty** to rule over the Korean peninsula. It remained in power until 935 C.E. This period in Korean history was one of great prosperity. The kingdom gained much new land and the population grew. There was also an increase in economic development. Unified Silla exported gold and silver goods and ginseng to China. It also imported books, ceramics, silks, clothes, and other items from Central and Southern Asia. Traders traveled on the **Silk Road** and by sea routes to the kingdom's ports.

Ports are places where ships load and unload goods. A main port in the Unified Silla Kingdom was in the present-day city of Hwaseong, found on the northwest coast of South Korea.

Later Three Kingdoms

After three centuries of rule, the Unified Silla Kingdom began to decline. People who lived within the kingdom were given a rank based on their descent. It was very hard for them to rise above the position they were assigned at birth. They demanded change. On top of that, many people believed the king had too much power and they were being forced to pay too many taxes. Several groups rebelled.

The country was divided into what became known as the Later Three Kingdoms: Koguryo, Paekche, and Silla. In 918 C.E., Wang Geon became the leader of the new Koguryo state, which he renamed Koryŏ. Eventually, the Unified Silla Kingdom surrendered to Wang Geon, and the Paekche kingdom soon followed.

Elaborate crowns from the Silla Kingdom were uncovered in the city of Gyeongju, the kingdom's former capital. Often made of gold, some had tiny dangling mirrors. Researchers believe the mirrors would reflect sunlight, symbolizing that the Silla kings who wore them represented the Sun on Earth.

After his death, Wang Geon was given the name King Taejo, which means Great Founder. The western name Korea was derived from the name Koryŏ.

Koryŏ Dynasty

After declaring himself king, Wang Geon vowed to unite the people once again. The Koryŏ Dynasty was very powerful. It enjoyed a favorable trade relationship with China, which exported silk, books, spices, tea, medicine, and ceramics to Koryŏ. Gold, silver, copper, ginseng, porcelain, pine nuts, and other goods were exported to China from Koryŏ. Japan sent swords and folding fans, while Arab traders brought ships filled with ivory, crystal, spices, amber, and mercury.

The Koryŏ Dynasty expanded the nation's boundaries. It established a unique culture that was unlike any other in East Asia. Hundreds of Buddhist temples and countless religious artworks were created under the orders of Koryŏ kings. However, in the 1200s, the Mongolian Empire invaded Koryŏ. It was the strongest power in the world at the time and very difficult to resist. It took control of the dynasty.

Chosŏn Dynasty

In 1392, a high-ranking Koryŏ military leader named Yi Song-gye overthrew the Koryŏ king and took his throne to form the Chosŏn Dynasty. It was the last Korean dynasty and the longest. It ruled from 1392 to 1910.

During the Chosŏn Dynasty, the country re-established its ties to China. It was therefore heavily influenced by Chinese culture and politics. **Confucianism** replaced Buddhism. It began to influence many traditions and ways of life that are still observed today. Farming became the main economy, and the Chosŏn Dynasty focused less on trade with other nations.

The Chosŏn Dynasty also placed a high importance on education. Many major scholarly accomplishments took place during this period. The Korean alphabet, called *Hangul*, was developed. Different Korean language **dialects** began to emerge, though most were universally understood.

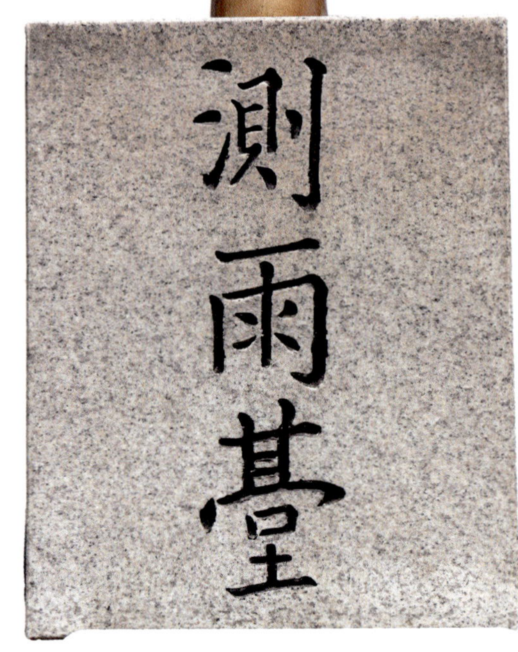

There were many scientific and technological advances during the Chosŏn Dynasty. These included the invention of devices for surveying the land, metal printing presses for book making, and the world's first rain gauge, shown here.

Hangul was invented during the reign of King Sejong, the Chosŏn Dynasty's fourth king. This statue in Seoul honors him.

Closer Look

Gyeongbokgung Palace, in modern-day Seoul, was the main royal palace of the Chosŏn Dynasty. It is an important cultural center today and houses two museums.

Chosŏn Capital

Yi Song-gye used feng shui to decide the location of the dynasty's new capital city. Feng shui is an ancient Chinese tradition that uses energy forces to balance humans and their environments. It involves placing buildings and other structures, such as tombs, in specific places. Yi therefore decided to locate the capital in the center of the Korean peninsula. It was called Hanyang. The Hangang, or Han, River flowed right through its core. This meant that the city was easily accessed by sea and by land. At the same time, the Han River valley provided fertile land for farming. Today, this city is known as Seoul.

Invasions and Seclusion

In 1592, Japan invaded Korea with the hope of eventually conquering China. After years of conflict, China helped Korea overcome Japan. But much of Korea had been devastated. Farmland, towns, temples, and palaces were destroyed. Skilled workers and **artisans** were taken captive. The Manchus also successfully attacked Korea twice, in the 1620s and 1630s. They were a **nomadic** people from northeast Asia. Though the Chosŏn Dynasty remained in power until 1910, its government was weak. Korea was largely cut off from all parts of the world, except China.

Fall of the Chosŏn Dynasty

Throughout the 1700s and 1800s, Korea recovered from its devastating attacks of the previous two centuries. Irrigation methods improved, and agriculture thrived as a result. The standard of living began to increase for everyone. By the mid-1800s, France, Great Britain, and the United States wanted to open up trade relations with Korea, but all were unsuccessful. The country remained in isolation until the 1880s.

Japan rallied to take full control of Korea and battled its neighbors for dominance. It defeated China in the Sino-Japanese War of 1894 to 1895, as well as Russia in the Russo-Japanese War of 1904 to 1905. In 1910, Japan **annexed** Korea, causing the Chosŏn Dynasty to fall.

The Manchus eventually took control of China as well. They established the Qing dynasty, which ruled China from 1644 to 1912. Qianlong (left) was the fifth emperor of this dynasty.

Because of its isolation from the rest of the world, Korea became known as a **hermit** kingdom during this period.

On this fence near the DMZ, South Koreans tie ribbons with messages to their estranged family members in North Korea. The North Korean government has occasionally allowed families to temporarily reunite, but most families are still separated.

Japanese Rule

Japan ruled Korea for the next 35 years. During this time, it tried to wipe out Korean culture and take land from the locals. Koreans were forced to speak Japanese, practice Japanese traditions, and even use Japanese names. In 1945, Japan's **colonial** rule ended. Following Japan's defeat in World War II, its territories, including Korea, were taken over by the **Allies**. Despite the end of the war, tensions were still high and Korea was divided along the 38th parallel. Russia occupied North Korea, while the United States occupied South Korea. In 1948, both countries established governments that claimed they represented the entire Korean peninsula. Two years later, war broke out between North and South Korea.

Closer Look

Korean War

In 1950, communist North Korea invaded democratic-capitalist South Korea. Russia and China both aided the North Korean forces. Other countries, led by the United States and backed by the **United Nations**, quickly lent their support to South Korea. The war raged for three years. There was mass destruction and millions of people died. A **ceasefire** was finally put in place, but the two Koreas remained divided along the DMZ. The war was devastating to people in the Korean peninsula. Between three and four million Koreans were killed—many being civilians. Millions of families were separated by the chaos of war and the DMZ.

Korea's industry and infrastructure was destroyed during the Korean War. Many Koreans lived in poverty in the years following the war.

CHAPTER 3

Life Today

South Korea is one of the fastest-growing economies in the world and one of the strongest in East Asia. Highly developed manufacturing and service industries are the top reasons for South Korea's wealth. But the country was not always the world leader it is today. In its early beginnings, South Korea went through a period of decline as one of the poorest countries in the world.

South Korea's economy ranks as the 12th most **productive** in the world.

Industrialization in Korea

Japan first brought **industrialization** to Korea in the 1920s and 1930s. By the end of World War II, Korea was the second-most industrialized nation in Asia after Japan. However, when Korea was divided, much of its manufacturing was located in North Korea. South Korea had to work hard to find ways to grow its economy.

Park Chung Hee ruled for nearly two decades before he was **assassinated** in 1979.

Strict Government Control

For more than three decades after the Korean War, South Korea was under strict **authoritarian** rule. The United States appointed Syngman Rhee as the first president of South Korea. However, he was forced to resign in 1960 due to his government's unfair treatment of citizens. Soon after, a military leader named Park Chung Hee took control of the government. The poverty-stricken country saw vast economic growth under Park, but he was a harsh **dictator**. He limited personal freedoms and rigged elections.

A New Way

Following Park, Chun Doo Hwan staged a **coup** and took control of the government. South Korea's economy grew about 10 percent each year under Chun. Still, the country remained under **authoritarian** rule and faced a great deal of political corruption. People began to protest. In 1987, Chun gave into demands for political freedom and free elections. He handpicked Roh Tae Woo to represent his ruling political party.

Roh was elected president and remained in power until 1993. During this time, a new constitution was put in place. Restrictions on individual freedoms were loosened. Today, South Korea is a **democratic republic**. It is led by a president, a prime minister, and a cabinet. The federal government has much less control over daily affairs. The country has flourished under this framework.

South Korea has evolved from a poor nation with limited prospects to one of the most powerful economies in the world. Its transformation has earned the nickname the "Miracle on the Han River."

Agriculture

In South Korea's early years, agriculture made up about 50 percent of its national wealth. By the 1980s, it accounted for only 15 percent. Today, it makes up less than 2 percent of the country's total economy. Only about 5 percent of people work in this industry, which includes farming, hunting, fishing, livestock production, and forestry.

Imports from other countries supply 70 percent of South Korea's food needs. This is due to an increase in **urbanization**, rising agricultural labor costs, and an aging rural labor force. Agricultural products in South Korea include rice, vegetables, cabbage, milk, onions, pork, poultry, eggs, mandarins, and potatoes.

These farmers are working in a rice field in southwest South Korea. Rice is a staple food and the most important crop in South Korea.

Since South Korea is surrounded by so much water, marine products are of great importance to the economy. The country is one of the largest seafood producers in the world.

Industry

Manufacturing, mining, construction, and electricity are some of the most important industries in South Korea. They make up about a third of the economy. About a quarter of the workforce is employed in these industries. The country produces automobiles, petrochemicals, clothing, footwear, electronics, shipbuilding, textiles, and steel products.

Other Sectors

About two-thirds of South Koreans work in the services sector. This sector includes medical care, tourism, banking, and education. It makes up nearly 60 percent of the nation's wealth. High-tech industries, such as electronics, bioengineering, and aerospace, are also massive businesses in South Korea.

Closer Look

During the COVID-19 pandemic, South Korea used technology, such as mandatory apps on smartphones, to track COVID spread, monitor outbreaks, and alert citizens. This kept cases and deaths relatively low in a country with densely populated cities.

Technology for Everyone

South Korea is one of the world's most technologically advanced and innovative countries. Contactless payments, 4D cinema, tablet computers, retina display, and touchscreen phones are just a few of the technologies that began in South Korea. About 98 percent of South Koreans have Internet access, which is one of the highest rates in the world. In addition, more than 90 percent of the population has a smartphone. People use their smartphones to pay at stores, watch real-time TV channels, and scan QR codes at the world's first virtual market.

Internet cafés, where Internet access is provided to the public, began in South Korea in 1988, before Internet was found in most homes.

Samsung, Hyundai, LG Electronics, and Kia are just a few of the innovative companies that call South Korea home.

Standard of Living

South Koreans enjoy a high standard of living. However, they work very hard, about 44 hours per week compared to the world average of just 32. They also sleep an average of just 6 hours a night. The average cost of living is about $1,100 per month, which is 1.5 times higher than the world average. Wages are fairly high due to the large skilled technology sector. After taxes, the average monthly salary is about $2,200, and there is a strong culture of saving and investing.

Bursting at the Seams

Shortages in housing, especially in the two major cities, Seoul and Pusan, have altered the landscape. The rapidly expanding population has led to more need for housing. But with a lack of land to build on, more high-rise towers have been built to accommodate this need. More than half of all Koreans live in an apartment.

Single-family homes are more common in rural areas where there is more land to build on.

Seoul is one of the most expensive cities in the world. A basic, one-bedroom apartment there costs about 975,000 South Korean Won ($840 USD) a month. However, compared to large U.S. cities, such as New York, it is still much more affordable. The average New Yorker, for example, pays about $3,900 a month.

Environmental Impact

Between 1960 and 1995, urbanization rose from about 36 percent to 85 percent. Sprawling development had a major impact on the environment, as green spaces were paved to make way for buildings and roads. Forests once covered about two-thirds of the country, for example, but they are now diminished. Emissions from automobiles and industries also began to take their toll on the environment. As a result, there is a lot of air pollution, acid rain, and water pollution in South Korea.

Planting trees in South Korea's cities can help combat air pollution and improve air quality.

Korea Train Express (KTX) is a high-speed railway that operates between Seoul and major cities such as Busan.

Airlines such as Korean Air and Asiana Airlines offer domestic service across South Korea as well as international flights.

Getting Around

A network of more than 68,307 miles (109,930 km) of roads connects cities and towns across the country. However, in crowded cities, traffic is a problem. Many people travel by subway or bus instead. Seoul is home to one of the longest and busiest subway systems on the planet. Most people travel by train between cities. About 2,000 miles (3,219 km) of railway lines links all parts of the country. Regional bus lines serve nearly every city and town in the country, big or small.

Waterways also form an important part of the transportation network. Some of the most important ports and harbors for international shipping are found in the cities of Chinhae, Incheon, Kunsan, Masan, Mokpo, Pohang, Ulsan, and Yosu. There are six domestic airports and eight international airports. Incheon International Airport, in Seoul, is one of the busiest in the world.

Closer Look

For an average high school student, classes start at 8 a.m. and run until about 4 p.m. After a short dinner break, most students study in the school library or with a private tutor.

South Korea's focus on education is credited in part for its economic and technological success.

Education

Few countries are as devoted to education as South Korea. The country has some of the highest education levels in the world as a result. Children aged 5 to 16 are required to attend school. They spend as many as 16 hours a day at school, or in after-school programs called *hagwons*.

The government funds a public education system that includes six years of primary school, three years of middle school, and three years of high school. Subjects include Korean language, social studies, mathematics, science, physical education, music, fine arts, and practical arts. Students begin learning English in the third grade. The school year is broken into two semesters: March through July and September through February.

CHAPTER 4

A Vibrant and Distinct Culture

Almost everyone who lives in South Korea is Korean. In fact, it's believed many are the direct descendants of some of the earliest ancient peoples to settle on the Korean peninsula. As a result, just about everyone shares one race and one culture. Traditional clothing, food, and ways of life are very similar across South Korea.

There is only a small foreign community in South Korea. It is made up mostly of people from China, Japan, and the United States. All South Koreans speak the Korean language, which uses the Hangul alphabet. There are several dialects, but they are all very similar. That means most people understand each other, no matter which dialect they speak.

Buddhist traditions, such as this performance, are an important part of South Korean culture. It has taken shape over thousands of years due to the various kingdoms and conflicts in the country.

Within families, the eldest son takes on greater responsibilities, including caring for his parents after they retire.

Religion

South Koreans have total religious freedom. They are allowed to practice any traditions or beliefs they want. Protestant is the most common religion, and it is practiced by nearly 20 percent of South Koreans. It is followed by Buddhism, at almost 16 percent. About 8 percent of people are Catholic, and approximately 57 percent do not practice any religion.

Though a small part of the population is Buddhist today, there are around 900 traditional Buddhist temples in South Korea. Many were built during the Three Kingdoms period, during which Buddhism was the main religion.

Confucianism

Confucianism is a worldview and way of life that focuses on personal **ethics**. It was developed by Confucius, a Chinese philosopher, in the 6th to 5th century B.C.E. Confucianism has been at the center of the South Korean way of life for hundreds of years. Many elements of it are present in daily life today.

A key part of Confucianism is respect for elders and ancestors. People often bow when they greet one another or say goodbye. Those who are well educated, work in a high-ranking job, or have achieved a certain social status also earn greater respect. South Koreans often ask people their age when they first meet so they can show an appropriate level of respect. They are also very formal around people who are not close friends or family members. They rarely address acquaintances or coworkers by their first names. Instead, they use different titles based on the person's age and relationship to them.

A baby's 100th day celebration is called *Baek-il*. South Korean parents still uphold this tradition today.

Milestone Events

Family is at the core of South Korean society and nothing is valued more. Many traditional celebrations and rituals mark important family-related milestones. For instance, in the past, babies did not often live past 100 days due to disease and starvation. They were kept away from outsiders while they built their **immunity**. On their 100th day, family and friends would greet them with gifts of gold and well wishes for a long and happy life. Other important milestones include a baby's first birthday, the 100-day anniversary of a new couple, a person's 61st birthday, and the anniversary of a person's death.

Festivals

Sŏllal is the first day of the Korean New Year. It is one of the most important holidays in South Korea, and celebrations last for three days. Another important celebration is the *Daeboreum*, or the Great Moon Festival. It commemorates the first full moon of the year. Since farming was such a big part of life in the past, many festivals celebrate this activity. *Hanshi*, or the Cold Food Festival, takes place 100 days after the **winter solstice**. It marks the beginning of the farming season. *Chusŏk* is a popular autumn holiday that honors the fall harvest. It is sometimes called Korean Thanksgiving.

Yeon Deung Hoe, or the Lotus Lantern Festival, is a spring celebration honoring the Buddha's birthday. People hang or carry colorful lotus lanterns and participate in cultural events and games.

Closer Look

Chinese Influence

Since its early beginnings, South Korean culture has been heavily influenced by the country's relationship with China. Aspects of Chinese culture can be seen in everything from architecture and art to government and religion. Even food, music, and clothing have their roots in Chinese culture. For instance, South Koreans built on the Chinese concept of using woodblocks for printing to create the world's first metal printing press. Another example is how South Korean potters have adapted the technique for making **celadon** into a style of pottery that was even more exquisite.

Traditional Korean art often depicts Chinese-style landscapes and portraits as well as Korean scenes and customs.

Celadon pottery was created during the Koryŏ dynasty.

Hanji covers the windows in this home. In addition to providing insulation and absorbing humidity, small holes in the paper provide **ventilation**.

Traditional Hanok

Traditional Korean homes are called *hanok*. These single-story houses are designed to showcase the most beautiful parts of the natural world around them. Where possible, they are built against a hill to increase sunlight and prevent cold winds. There is usually a stream or river nearby that provides access to water.

Hanok are built with *ondol*, a type of underfloor heating developed thousands of years ago in the country's cold northern regions. Hanok also have *maru*, a cool wooden floor that acts as a form of natural air conditioning. Maru was developed in the country's warm, southern regions. *Hanji*, a traditional Korean paper, covers every flat surface inside the hanok. It provides excellent insulation and absorbs humidity. It also allows sunlight to shine through.

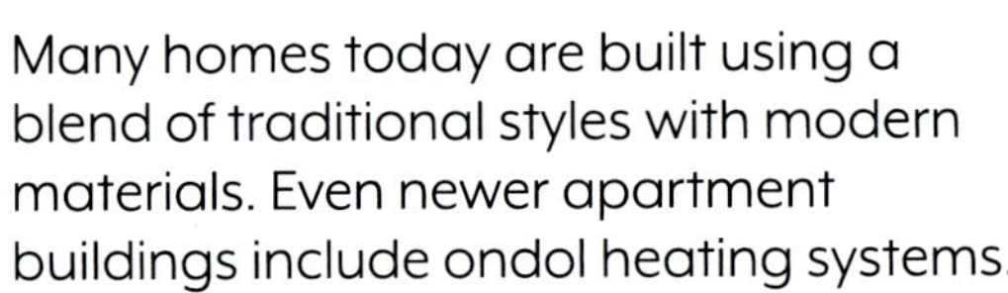

Many homes today are built using a blend of traditional styles with modern materials. Even newer apartment buildings include ondol heating systems.

Modern Housing

In crowded South Korean cities, every square foot counts when looking for a place to live. Most Koreans today live in sky-rise apartment complexes made up of about 8 to 16 buildings. Each building stands about 5 to 20 stories high, and the entire complex is surrounded by shopping centers, sports facilities, daycares, and other services. Outside of cities, where there is more land, people may live in more spacious detached houses. They are often very expensive.

Hanbok is designed with a slim-fitting top and a wider bottom to allow more graceful movement—making it seem as if the wearer is floating.

Children traditionally wear brightly colored *hanbok*, especially overcoats.

Clothing

Many South Koreans wear Western-style clothing, except for special occasions, such as weddings or festivals. Traditional clothing is called ***hanbok***. It includes a shirt with a long, wide skirt for women or pants for men. People wear different colors of hanbok depending on the occasion or their social status. For instance, people in higher social positions wear bright colors. Adults in a lower social position, on the other hand, wear plain clothes in muted tones.

Traditional South Korean clothing is beautiful, but it's also practical so that it stands up to extreme weather conditions. ***Sambe***, or hemp, and ***mosi***, or ramie, a type of grass, are used to make cool summer clothes. Cotton **wadding** was sewn between two pieces of cloth, such as silk or cotton, to make warm winter clothing.

On average, South Koreans consume 129 pounds (58.4 kg) of seafood per person each year. This is more than any other country in the world.

Food and Dining

South Koreans value healthy eating and believe food is the best medicine. Rice is the main dish, and it is usually accompanied by side dishes, such as kimchi, vegetable, and soup. Fish and other seafood are staple foods and readily available since South Korea is so close to the ocean.

Table manners are very important, and there are some basic rules South Koreans follow at mealtimes. For instance, older people should always be seated first, and younger people should never pick up their tableware before their elders. After digging in, everyone should try to eat at the same pace.

Closer Look

Kimchi

Kimchi is a type of spicy, **fermented** vegetable. It is the most important food in South Korea, and it is included as a side dish at every meal. It is rich in nutrients and very healthy. Traditionally, women would spend several days making kimchi each November or December so there would be enough to last throughout the winter. They used a special process to preserve kimchi for months or even years. Today, most people buy kimchi at the store, but some still make their own, especially rural families.

There are about 100 types of kimchi, such as cabbage, radish, and cucumber. There is even a national museum dedicated to it.

Kimchi is fermented in onggi pots.

The *Namsadang Nori*, pictured here, is a traditional folk performance that includes music, dancing, acting, acrobatics, and puppets.

Music and Dance

Pansori is a type of traditional folk music that dates back to the 1600s. It is a form of storytelling that is performed by a singer and a drummer. Performances can last up to eight hours and include dancers or narrators. *Pungmul* is another type of traditional singing and drumming that also includes dances and acrobatics. Farmers would perform it after a long day of work. It is common to see *pungmul* at festivals and special events.

Korean popular music, or K-Pop, refers to any form of mainstream music, such as rock, hip hop, and techno. It became widespread in the 1990s and is now popular around the world. Well-known K-Pop artists include BoA, Exo, BTS, and Wonder Girls.

The 2012 song "Gangnam Style" by South Korean singer Psy, pictured left alongside his background dancers, was an international hit.

CHAPTER 5

Looking to the Future

From the work people do to the clothes they wear and the houses they build, South Koreans have tailored their ways of life around their physical geography. This has been a practice throughout history. However, South Korea's physical geography has also changed as a result of human activities.

Impact of Growth

Massive development in the 1960s and 1970s quickly improved the country's poor economic situation after the Korean War. By the 1990s, South Korea was one of the most advanced, wealthiest nations. However, a period of mass population growth and extreme urbanization accompanied this economic shift. Green spaces dwindled as more land was needed for apartments and businesses. **Carbon emissions** rose significantly, and air and water quality were greatly affected.

South Korea's rapid urbanization has meant that cities have expanded drastically, **encroaching** on the surrounding environment.

Reducing the Impact

While South Koreans are taking steps to reduce the impact of such rapid growth on the country, it will take years to undo the damage. By understanding the past and present conditions of their country as well as their relationship with the land, South Koreans can better plan for the future. They can make informed decisions about urban planning, climate initiatives, and other aspects of their daily lives.

A Smaller Carbon Footprint

Air pollution is expected to become the top environmental cause of early death by the year 2050. The main causes of air pollution are transportation and the burning of wood or coal. The government plans to become **carbon neutral** by 2050. It's an ambitious plan that requires the country to quickly ramp up clean technologies and renewable energy sources.

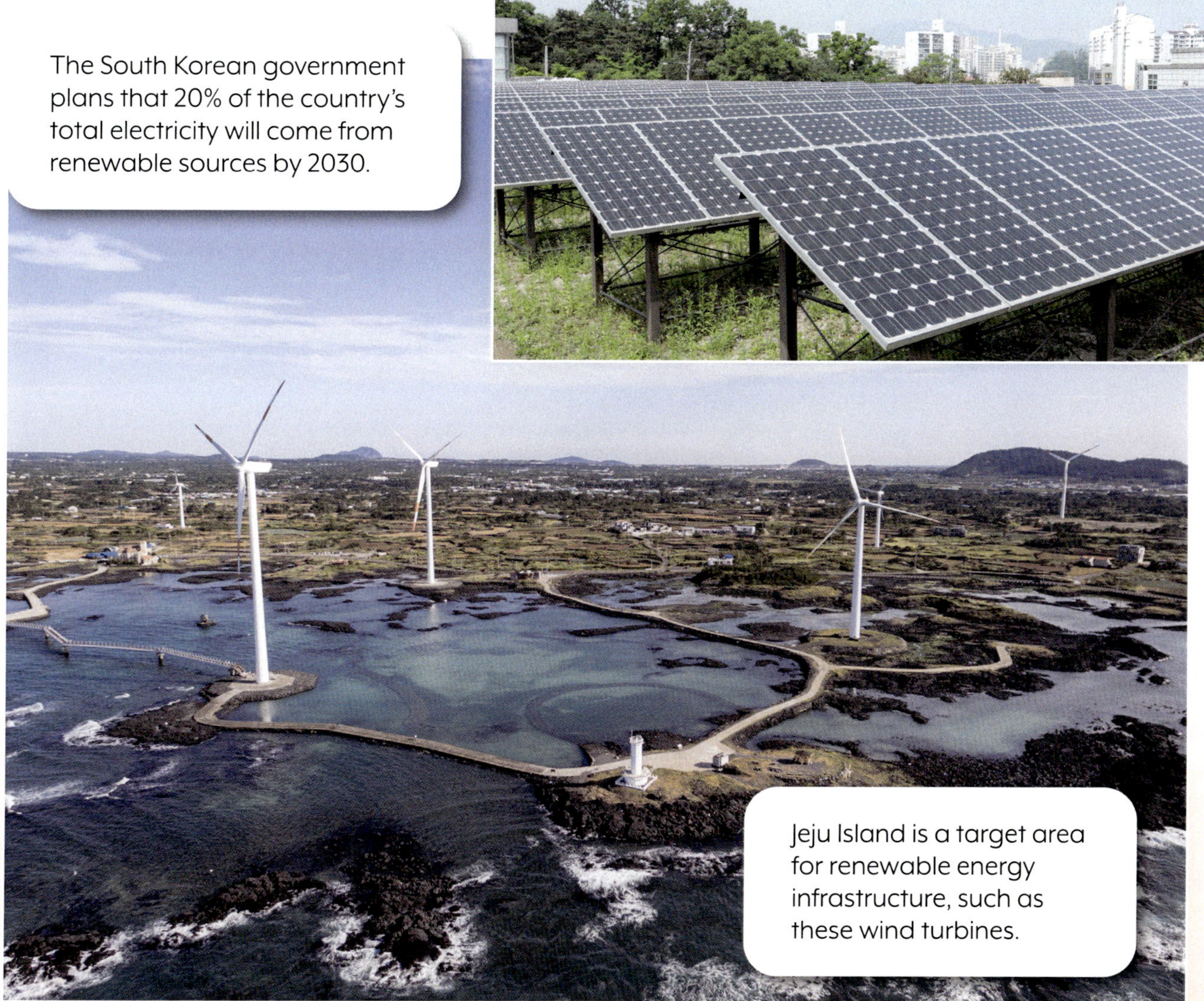

The South Korean government plans that 20% of the country's total electricity will come from renewable sources by 2030.

Jeju Island is a target area for renewable energy infrastructure, such as these wind turbines.

Going Forward

South Korea is working to build green growth initiatives. Its major environmental projects aim to improve quality of life and reduce climate changes. The country has made impressive progress since the 1990s and now serves as an example to other countries around the world. A first step was the creation of a greenbelt around Seoul in the 1970s. It accounts for about 13.3 percent of the Seoul metropolitan area and has helped limit urban sprawl. There is no longer a way for the city to grow outward, only upward.

The greenbelt has helped improve air control and water supply and quality, but it has led to more congestion within the city limits.

The Songdo International Business District focuses on eco-friendly transportation, such as bicycles, and has an automatic waste collection and disposal system.

Smart Cities

One of the ways South Korea is looking to become a more efficient and sustainable country is through eco-friendly initiatives and projects that use leading-edge technologies to make lives easier and greener. The Songdo International Business District in Incheon was designed with energy efficiency in mind. LED streetlights, solar energy supplies, **geothermal** heating and cooling facilities, and rainwater storage facilities are just a few of the energy-saving features in this district.

Increased precipitation due to climate change puts Seoul more at risk for extreme flooding. The government is planning to reduce the impact of flooding on citizens with solutions such as installing rainwater storage tanks and retrofitting areas with pavement that allows better drainage.

Looking Ahead

Seoul has come up with an urban planning approach that looks ahead over the next 100 years. It includes preserving places of cultural, historical, and ecological importance and building communities that reduce the distance between where people live and work. Seoul will also introduce more public transportation systems to reduce traffic congestion and pollution. The city will look for sustainable development and renewable energy platforms to reduce environmental damage. It will also use smart technologies to become more efficient.

Path Forward

In July 2020, the South Korean government announced the Korean New Deal: National Strategy for a Great Transformation. It consists of three parts. First, the Digital New Deal focuses on building a smart country based on data, networks, and **artificial intelligence** infrastructure. Next, the Green New deal looks at creating balance between humans and the natural environment while moving toward a goal of zero **greenhouse gas** emissions. Finally, Stronger Safety Net aims to provide more jobs, better social services, and create a more secure future for all South Koreans.

Unifying the Two Koreas

Reunifying North and South Korea could result in benefits for both countries. South Korea's manufacturing sector currently relies on imports of raw materials. In a reunified country, these resources could be provided by resource-rich North Korea. North Koreans, on the other hand, could possibly gain access to better healthcare and other services by reuniting with South Korea. However, upgrading infrastructure and programs to bring these services to all people would come at a huge cost. There are also many challenges standing in the way of reunification. Differences in government and other systems mean both countries have very unique perspectives on the future.

Issues in North Korea, such as nuclear weapons production, human rights violations, and poor foreign relations, also make reunification of the Korean peninsula unlikely in the near future.

Declining Population

In recent years, South Korea's population has started to rapidly decline. Many people are choosing not to start a family due to the rising cost of living and lack of employment opportunities. The shrinking population is a major concern for a country that needs a vast workforce to continue its economic growth. Since the country is still in conflict with North Korea, it also needs plenty of recruits to enroll in its military programs. One way South Korea is addressing the issue is through the use of emerging technologies, such as robot workers and self-driving military vehicles. South Korea is also encouraging women and seniors to play a bigger role in the labor force.

An easing of immigration restrictions would mean more foreign workers could join the South Korean workforce.

The South Korean government has taken measures to make it easier for citizens to have children. They include longer parental leaves when a new child is born and better childcare programs so both parents can work outside the home.

The government will need to focus on supporting the senior population with policies such as income support, safe housing and health care, and active community involvement in retirement.

An Aging Population

Another population concern is the increase in senior citizens. This is partly due to the fact that South Koreans are living longer. Improved life expectancy has led to a big increase in the amount of healthcare spending, as older people often require more care. By increasing the retirement age from 55 to 60, the government hoped older people would work longer. However, it meant fewer jobs for people under the age of 30.

Meeting Challenges

Since the Korean War, South Korea has worked hard to shed its image as a poor, defenseless country. Despite the many challenges of the past, South Koreans have made the most of their rugged landscape. Today, South Korea's economy is thriving. As one of the most innovative countries in the world, the country is well positioned to confront the issues of increasing productivity in a slower economy, address the issues of an aging and declining population, and reduce environmental impacts.

38th parallel A name given to the latitude 38 degrees north of the equator, on which the Korean peninsula is divided

alliances Agreements to work together

Allies Countries, including the U.S., Canada, and France, that fought together against the Axis powers, including Germany and Japan

annexed Took control of an area and added it to a larger area

artificial intelligence The ability of a computer to solve problems and make decisions like humans

artisans Workers in skilled trades, especially those who make things by hand

assassinated Killed for political or religious reasons

authoritarian A form of government in which personal freedoms are limited and submission to authority is required

capitalist A system in which individuals can hold wealth and control the production of goods

carbon emissions Releases of carbon into the atmosphere. Carbon is a chemical element. Carbon compounds such as carbon dioxide contribute to climate change.

carbon neutral Not emitting more carbon than is absorbed

ceasefire An agreement to stop fighting

celadon Pottery that is glazed in the celadon green color

collectivist culture A society in which group needs are prioritized over individual ones

colonial Relating to a colony, or a country or area occupied by and under the control of another country

colonization The process by which a country takes control of another country or area by occupying it

communist A system in which the government controls the production of goods and wealth is shared among citizens

confederation A union of independent states

Confucianism A way of life and worldview based on the teachings of Chinese philosopher Confucius

coup Violent overthrow of a government

democratic republic A form of government that combines a republic, in which a country is ruled by elected representatives, and a democracy, in which the power is with citizens

densely Gathered closely

desertification The process by which fertile land becomes desert, often due to drought and improper land use

dialects Forms of languages that are specific to a region or group

dictator A ruler with total power over a country

dynasty A family of rulers in which power is passed down

economy The production and consumption of goods in a country

encroaching Intruding on

eroded Gradually wore away

ethics Ideas about right or wrong that influence behavior

fermented Of an organic substance, underwent a chemical change

fertile Able to produce crops

fortified Made stronger

geothermal Relating to heat that comes from the earth

ginseng A plant often used in medicines

graphite A gray mineral often used in manufacturing

greenhouse gas Gases, such as carbon dioxide, that trap heat in Earth's atmosphere

hermit Living in solitude

immunity Ability to keep from becoming infected

industrialization The process by which an area or country changes from mostly agricultural to more industry-based, focused on manufacturing goods

levees Ridges built up along a river to stop flooding

metropolitan Relating to a large city and its surrounding area

nomadic Moving from place to place

ore Rock that contains valuable minerals

productive Producing large amounts of goods

reforestation The process of replanting trees in an area

respiratory Relating to the lungs or breathing

Silk Road A network of trade routes connecting China and other eastern countries with Europe

storm surge Severe rise in seawater during a storm

tribal states Self-governed nations of people with shared ancestry

tungsten A chemical element often used to make steel stronger or in light bulbs

United Nations An international organization founded in 1945 to promote world peace and security

urbanization The process by which an area or country changes from mostly rural to more urban, with more cities

ventilation Providing fresh air to an indoor space

wadding A soft, thick material used to line clothing or protect fragile items

winter solstice The day that marks the start of winter, when either of Earth's poles is tilted the furthest from the Sun on its axis and there is the shortest amount of daylight

World Heritage Site A protected landmark or area singled out by UNESCO as being globally significant

Books

Bowler, Ann Martin. *All About Korea: Stories, Songs, Crafts and Games for Kids.* Tuttle Publishing, 2018.

Kang, Woosung. *Korean Culture Dictionary: From Kimchi To K-Pop And K-Drama Clichés. Everything About Korea Explained!* New Ampersand Publishing, 2021.

Keller, Tae. *When You Trap a Tiger.* Random House Books for Young Readers, 2020.

Websites

Learn more about living in South Korea.
www.oecdbetterlifeindex.org/countries/korea

Explore Korean culture, from UNESCO World Heritage Sites to food and art, on the Korean Cultural Center website.
www.koreanculture.org

Find out more facts about South Korea.
www.cia.gov/the-world-factbook/countries/korea-south

About the Author

Heather C. Hudak has written hundreds of kids' books on all kinds of topics. She loves to travel when she's not writing. Heather has visited about 60 countries and hopes to travel to South Korea one day.